BECCA THE BANANA'S BRUISED BUTT!

Words & pictures by
Glenn Madigan

Dedicated to my adventurous nephews,
Andrew & Ivan.

Becca the Banana is trying something new.

She's going to the skate park to attempt her biggest trick yet – "The Banana Split."

BUTTER

It will take speed.
It will take skill.
And it will take bravery.

Becca is ready.

With a push on her skateboard,
she zooms across the ground,
closer and closer to the ramp.

3... 2... 1...

She's in the air!
She reaches for her board,
but she misses, and tumbles!

Down,
down,
down,
OUCH!

What's that? A bruise!

BECCA BRUISED HER BUTT!

GASP!

She walks home and
finds her Nana.

"What's wrong, dear?" asks her Nana.
"I tried a new trick and failed," explains Becca,
"Now I'm sad and bruised."

"My sweet Becca – you'll try many new things in life, and you may not always succeed."

"But even when you fail, you'll learn something new and will use that to become better at whatever you set your mind to."

In that moment, Becca notices that
her Nana has many bruises, just like hers.

"Our bruises are badges – a sign of taking risks. This may be your first, but it won't be your last. How you grow from each bruise is what matters most of all."

19

The next morning,
Becca is ready
to try again.

All of her friends follow her
to the skate park.

BECCA

Elbow pads... Check!

Knee pads... All set!

Helmet... Click!

Skateboard... Ready!

She pushes off on her board
and is once again zooming
through the air.

Faster... and faster...

...and faster!

up!

up,

Up,

Here comes the ramp.

28

Becca reaches for her board...

it's the banana split!
BECCA

She flips and lands.
Back on her board.
Back on the ground.

She did it!

Becca is so proud of herself for trying again
and for succeeding at something new.

She knows now that taking risks and
ending up with a bruise is better
than never trying at all.

BECCA

Now it's time to plan
her next trick.